Art Director	Charles Matheson
Art Editor	Ben White
Editor	Mike March
Illustrators	Chris Forsey
	Hayward Art Group
	Jim Robins
	Julie Stiles

© Aladdin Books Ltd

Designed and produced by
Aladdin Books Ltd
70 Old Compton Street
London W1

*First published in the
United States 1982 by*
Franklin Watts
730 Fifth Avenue
New York
New York 10019

ISBN 531-04582-X
Library of Congress
Catalog Card No: 82-50857

Franklin Watts Science World

Geology

Dougal Dixon

Series Editor: Lionel Bender

FRANKLIN WATTS
London · Toronto · New York · Sydney

Introduction

Geology is the study of the Earth, from the rocks and the soil of the surface to the mysteries of the distant inner core.

In this book we first examine how the Earth was made thousands of millions of years ago, and how this process still affects the surface and interior today. The only part that we can study directly is the crust, but this is the part, although it looks very solid and stable, that is constantly moving. The results of this can be seen in the growth of mountains, and in the folding and cracking of rock layers, as well as in earthquakes and volcanoes.

The different kinds of rocks affected by this movement have been formed in different ways. Some have solidified after molten rocky material has been squeezed up from deep below the crust; others have been built up from layers of sand and mud that have been cemented together. These rocks, as we shall discover, are all made of minerals, each having a distinct chemical composition.

With even the continents constantly changing position, their climates have changed, and animal and plant life has developed from microscopic sea-living organisms to the thousands of different species we see around us today. We know all this because of fossil traces found in the rocks, and the techniques geologists use to interpret them.

Finally, the book examines the importance of geology in the wider context of modern-day society: how dependent we are on geological substances and, indeed, how our whole lives are governed by the Earth's processes.

Five thousand million years ago the Earth's surface was a bubbling molten mass. Very gradually, as it cooled and the gases in the air began to form water, life on Earth began. At first this took the form of algae breeding in hot springs. Only 400 million years ago did the first creatures crawl onto land. But the science of geology not only tells us a lot about the past; and how our planet came to be the way it is today; it can also uncover important mineral resources and fuel deposits essential to our way of life.

5,000 million years ago

Life's beginnings

Contents

Life develops on Earth

Mining mineral resources

The Earth

Can you imagine viewing our own planet, Earth, from space? The American, Neil Armstrong, one of the first men to travel to the Moon, described it as "a beautiful jewel in space." From high above the Earth you can make out the shapes of the continents and the blue expanses of the oceans, but most, of the fine details are hidden by the haze of the atmosphere and the white, fluffy cloud masses hovering above the Earth's surface. The sparkling array of blues, greens, and browns visible through the shifting patterns of bright cloud is probably as fine a spectacle as can be seen anywhere in the Solar System. The oceans are restless, too, and even our continents move – although very slowly, and so much less obviously. But it is these movements that create our land patterns and form the great mountain ranges.

▷ Seen from space, Earth is a globe, spinning on its axis and shimmering in its atmosphere. Banks of cloud, rising to about 13 km (8 miles) above the surface, change their patterns by the hour.

The Earth's surface
Certain early cultures believed that everything was made up of fire, water, earth and air. Looking at the Earth's surface, it is easy to see why.

Atmosphere

Land

Sea

From satellite photographs it can be seen that the ratio of water to land on the Earth's surface is about three to one. But what we see is only on the crust, a thin rind covering the Earth's globe. Beneath the crust our planet is built up of different layers, rather like an onion. Some of these layers are solid, some liquid and some, in part, are both. There are currents in the liquid, as you would see in milk or jam heated in a saucepan, that cause the different layers to move over each other, pushing the crust and the continents into their various positions.

Since it became possible to gather information from space probes, we have greatly improved our knowledge of the workings of our planet. Measurements taken from orbit, and satellite pictures, have helped us to discover just what the Earth's surface is made of, how it moves and how it came to be what it is today. This has led, in turn, to the discovery of new deposits of valuable minerals, and benefited agriculture by identifying regions suitable for growing specialist crops. All these studies are part of the science of geology – the science of the Earth.

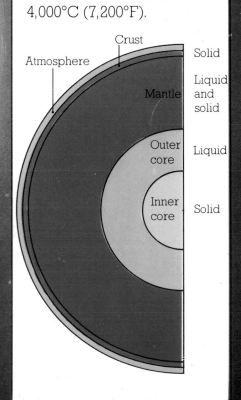

Section through the Earth
Earth has an inner and outer core, made mostly of iron, and then a mantle. The temperature rises according to depth, and at the Earth's center is believed to be 4,000°C (7,200°F).

Atmosphere

Crust

Mantle

Outer core

Inner core

Solid

Liquid and solid

Liquid

Solid

Origin of the Earth

The cloud condenses

Scientists believe that the Solar System began about 10,000 million years ago as a huge cloud of cold dust and gas, which then started to close in on itself. As it did so, it flattened out into a disk and began to spin. The spinning was fastest at the center, where dust particles built up into lumps and grew bigger and bigger. This was the origin of our Sun.

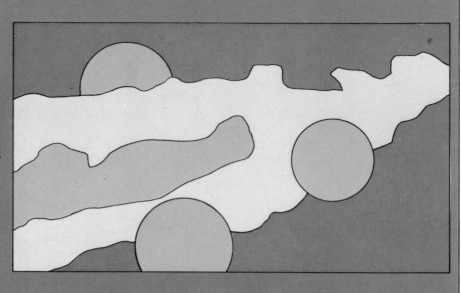

The Solar System forms

As more and more matter fell into the Sun, it became hotter. Meanwhile, away from the center of the disk, the dust and gas began to break up into eddies. There, too, matter started to collect, drawing in more dust as its mass and gravitational force increased. This was the beginning of our planetary system. About 5,000 million years ago, the Solar System became like it is today.

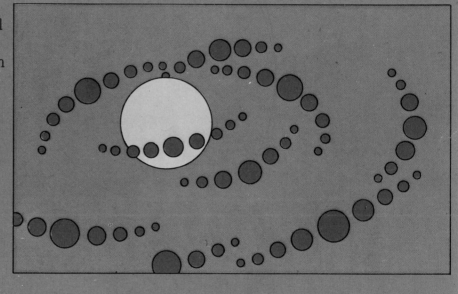

The Earth as a fiery ball

The formation of the planets was complete, and there was very little free dust and gas left in-between. The planets closest to the Sun are mainly rocky bodies, the outer planets are made mostly of gas. Our planet, Earth, heated up as it condensed. The surface rapidly cooled to form the crust, but much of the interior stayed hot and molten.

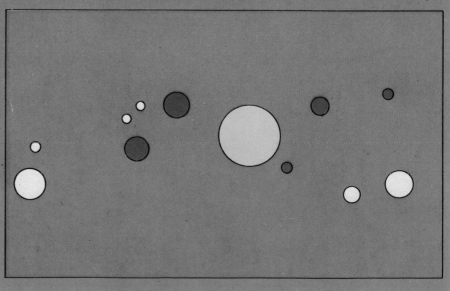

Volcanoes

The Earth's surface is not completely stable. During a violent earthquake or volcanic eruption it can be seen to move. The molten rock that pours out of a volcano comes from below the Earth's surface. Hot material is slowly moving about in the mantle all the time. Sometimes it finds a weak spot in the crust where it can break through. After it has erupted it solidifies. This is how volcanoes were formed, and this is why some are still active today.

Volcanoes are mostly found at the edges, or in the middle, of the oceans. There, the crust is at its thinnest – sometimes only 10 km (6.2 miles), compared with 35 km (22 miles) underneath land.

Volcano

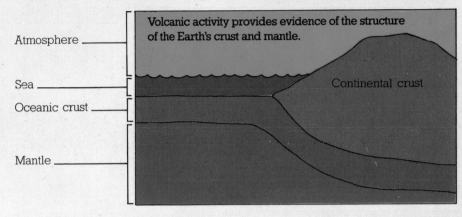

Volcanic activity provides evidence of the structure of the Earth's crust and mantle.

Atmosphere

Sea

Oceanic crust

Mantle

Continental crust

Earthquakes

Generally, the movements of the Earth's crust are too slow to be noticed. But sometimes they are very sudden, resulting in earthquakes. Earth tremors produce different kinds of shock waves. So-called P-waves travel through solids and liquids, whereas S-waves travel only through solids. P-waves are about twice as fast as S-waves. As they pass through the different layers of the Earth, the waves are bent to varying degrees. This is known as refraction. By studying these wave patterns scientists can learn a lot about the interior of the Earth.

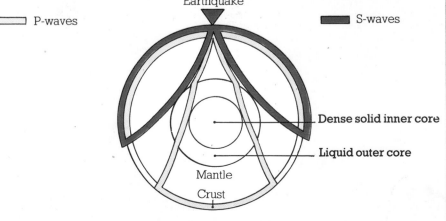

Earthquake

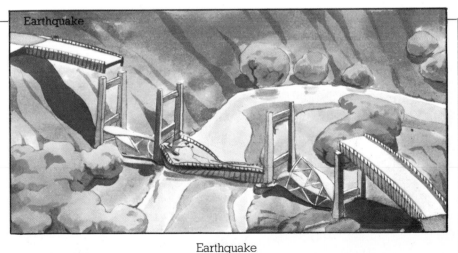

▭ P-waves

Earthquake

■ S-waves

Dense solid inner core

Liquid outer core

Mantle

Crust

9

The Moving Crust

Why is it that the Earth's crust is always moving? Iceland will serve as an example. Iceland is a large island in the North Atlantic consisting almost entirely of volcanoes. Every so often, one of these erupts, bringing new material to the surface, from the mantle. On the surface it hardens and becomes part of the crust. So new crust is always being formed in Iceland.

But Iceland is by no means the only place where this happens. If you look at a map of the world you will see that Iceland lies on a submarine ridge that runs from north to south along the length of the Atlantic Ocean. Similar ridges can be found in other oceans of the world. Underwater volcanoes are erupting all the time along these ocean ridges, and so the crust is being constantly replenished by new molten material raised from the mantle. In fact, the whole surface of the Earth consists of slabs, or plates, of crust that are constantly growing from the ocean ridges.

What happens when two plates growing in opposite directions meet head on? The same thing that happens when two ice-floes are pushed together: one is forced downward and the other slides over it. The plate that is forced downward melts into the mantle, and the process begins again. This occurs when there are deep troughs in the ocean bed. The continents are not driven under in this way. Although their crust is much thicker than the ocean crust, it is also much lighter. In fact, the continents are carried about in the ocean crust like logs frozen into ice-floes.

The movement of the crustal plates is slow, only a few inches each year. From this, geologists have deduced that nowhere is the ocean floor more than 140 million years old.

▽ Iceland and its neighboring islands have been built up over about 50 million years of volcanic activity. Volcanoes and earthquake zones are mainly found at the plate boundaries, where the crust is the least stable.

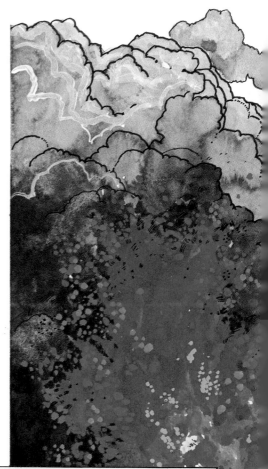

Producing new crust
The new material that is pushed up from the mantle is in the form of vertical sheets, called "dikes". In contact with sea water, these cool to become underwater volcanoes. As these erupt, the material moves outward.

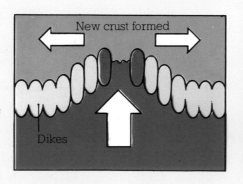

New crust formed

Dikes

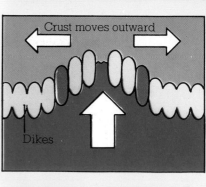

Crust moves outward

Dikes

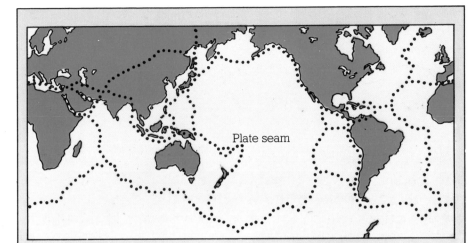

Crustal plates

The Earth's surface consists of plates, like panels on a football. Each panel is growing along one seam and being destroyed along another. At the seams lie volcanoes. This phenomenon is known as plate tectonics.

Plate seam

The Changing World

Geologists can learn a lot about the movement of continents, and how they change their shape, by studying rocks. In Northern Europe, particularly Scotland, red sandstones with entire sand dunes preserved in them are by no means uncommon. They could have only been made in hot desert – so local climates in the distant past must have been very different from what they are today!

Rock record – present day

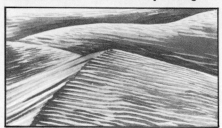
Scottish desert – 250 million years ago

Three hundred and fifty million years ago what is now the British Isles lay south of the Equator, in the Southern Desert belt. Over the next 50 million years they drifted north to the Equator, and supported lush, tropical forests. The movement northward continued, through the Northern Desert belt, until they reached where they are today. The Earth's crustal movements will keep going indefinitely.

The Restless Earth

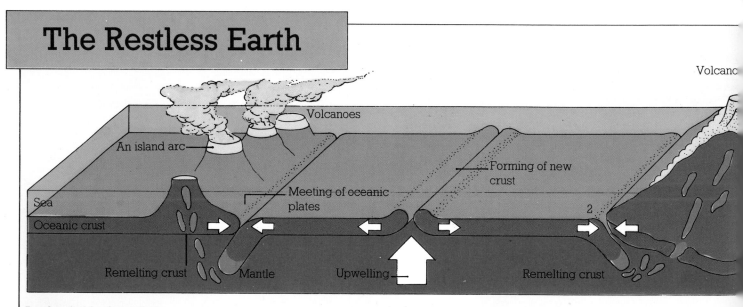

Volcano

Volcanoes

An island arc

Forming of new crust

Sea

Oceanic crust

Meeting of oceanic plates

2

Remelting crust

Mantle

Upwelling

Remelting crust

A volcanic island arc: *Japan*

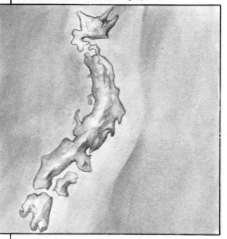

When two ocean plates collide, blobs of molten crust from the plate that has sunk into the mantle rise to the surface by forcing their way upward through the other plate (1). This is how chains of volcanic islands are formed. Japan is typical of the arc-shaped island chains of the Western Pacific. The South Sandwich Islands, in the South Atlantic, are another example.

An ocean plate sinking beneath a plate carrying a continent (2) will crumple the edge of the continent to form a mountain range. The Andes and the Rockies were made in this way. Sometimes the molten material from the sinking plate will push up through the mountains to produce volcanoes, such as Mount St. Helens, Washington, in the USA.

The Earth's changing face

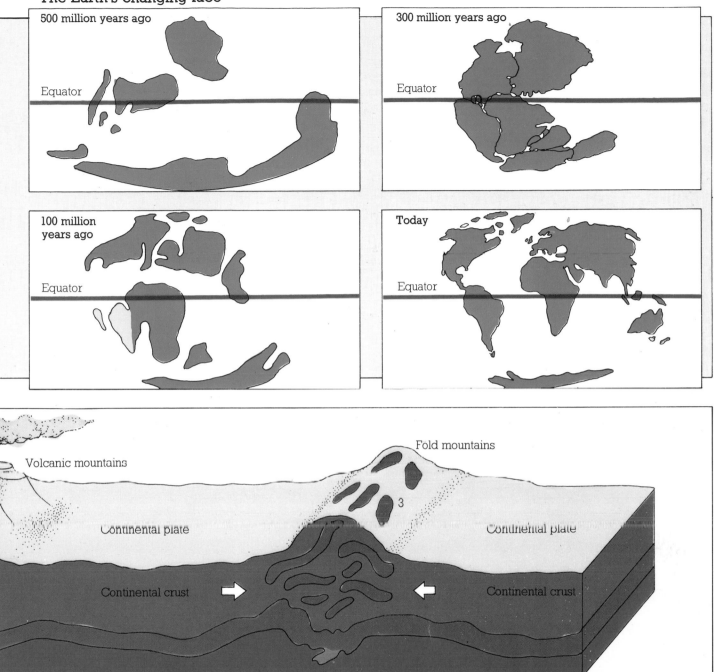

500 million years ago

Equator

300 million years ago

Equator

100 million years ago

Equator

Today

Equator

Fold mountains

Volcanic mountains

Continental plate

Continental crust

Continental plate

Continental crust

3

Volcanic mountains: *The Andes*

When two plates both carrying continents meet, neither one is drawn down into the mantle. Instead they weld together, with enormous mountains forming along the join (3). An example of such "fold" mountains is the Himalayas, formed when two huge continent-carrying plates collided, and the edges where they met rose under the impact.

Fold mountains: *The Himalayas*

Folds

If you push together the opposite edges of a pile of papers, the sheets bulge upward in the middle. The same thing happens with layers of rock. When they are pushed together by gigantic mountain-building movements, they are forced into folds.

In nature, folds in rocks can be tiny, or alternatively they can form whole mountain chains. Similarly, the folds may be very shallow or they may be very steep. Sometimes the force exerted by one side of the fold can turn the fold right over (overthrust).

"Mountain building"

Types of fold

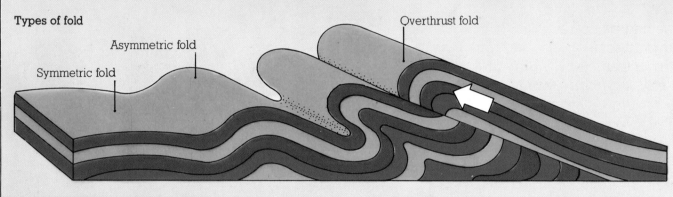

Symmetric fold

Asymmetric fold

Overthrust fold

Faults

Sometimes rock layers that are pushed or pulled cannot fold, but crack and shift instead. These cracks are called faults. Along a fault the rocks may move just a few inches or they may shift so far that whole continents are displaced.

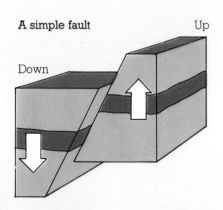

A simple fault

Up

Down

The San Andreas fault in California is part of a system stretching from Mexico to Alaska. To the west of it the land moves northward in a series of earthquake zones. The African Rift Valley was formed when two continents separated and the middle part sank between the faults.

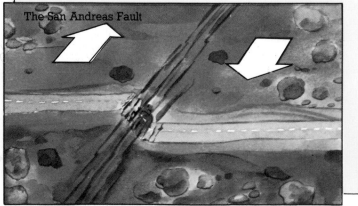

The San Andreas Fault

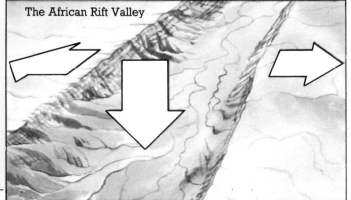

The African Rift Valley

Shaping the Mediterranean

The original situation

Spain

EUROPE

Italy

Mediterranean Sea

AFRICA

Plate movements

Mountains

Volcanoes

Earthquakes

Europe moving West

Alps

Italy

Pyrenees mountains

Spain

Atlas mountains

Africa moving East

The Mediterranean plates

Folding and faulting are taking place on a truly grand scale in the Mediterranean, where Africa is slowly moving against Southern Europe. Some day, there may be no Mediterranean Sea, but a new mountain range will have taken its place.

As the African and European crustal plates began to come together, the rock layers of the seabed in-between were folded into mountains. Today, these are the Atlas Mountains and the Alps. Italy, where today there is still volcanic activity, was twisted into its present shape, and Spain swung round from its original position in the Bay of Biscay. The Pyrenees were thrown up where the land bent, and Sardinia and Corsica were pulled away from the French coast. On the island of Crete, in the Eastern Mediterranean, the Minoan civilization was totally destroyed, 2,500 years ago, by a massive volcano – a result of the crustal movements.

The Pyrenees – Mountain forming

Mount Etna – Volcano

Italy – Earthquake

15

Hard Rocks

When geologists talk about hard rocks they mean rocks that have solidified from a "hot melt:" they have been affected by great heat and pressure deep down in the Earth's crust. The hot liquid produced when parts of the crust melt at great depths is known as magma. Sometimes the magma is forced up to the surface, or into the higher layers of the crust, where it cools and hardens. Hard rocks formed in this way are called igneous rocks.

New igneous rocks are found at the edges of the crustal plates, in areas of mountain-building and volcanic activity. Older igneous rocks, however, are found all over the world, indicating that centers of activity have shifted over the ages.

Another kind of hard rock is formed when existing rocks are heated or squeezed by the Earth's movements. New chemical compounds or minerals are produced in the rocks themselves, making them heavier or lighter, changing their texture and appearance – in short, transforming them into completely new rocks. These rocks are known as metamorphic rocks.

▷ Devil's Tower, in Wyoming, US, is a cylindrical mass of igneous rock dominating the surrounding countryside. It was formed by magma solidifying in a vertical tube that was once the heart of a volcano.

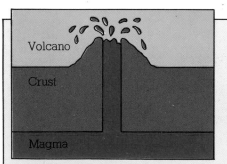
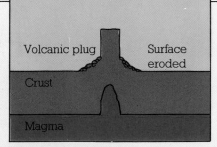

Hard rock resisting erosion

Magma forcing its way up through the crust and spilling over eventually produces a familiar cone-shaped volcano. After the eruption has ceased, the weather wears away the volcano and surrounding rock, leaving just the hard core, or plug.

Not all metamorphic rocks look the same. Those formed mostly by heat, such as marble, tend to resemble igneous rocks, while those that are formed under pressure have a stretched or twisted appearance, showing the stresses and strains undergone in their formation.

Most hard rocks, igneous and metamorphic, are formed deep underground, well away from where we can see them. They may eventually appear at the surface, when they are millions of years old, but only after the rocks above them have been worn away.

It is not difficult to distinguish hard rocks in a landscape. They tend to form hills that protrude above the surrounding flat scenery. This is because they are less easily broken down or worn away by wind and rain than the softer rocks, and so remain standing for longer periods. But they too will eventually undergo the same process of erosion. When that happens their fragments will be washed away in streams and rivers to accumulate in another place where they will be reformed into yet another sort of rock.

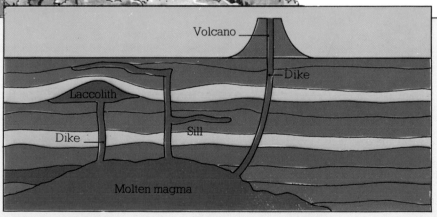

Volcanic features

When magma solidifies it can result in a number of structural features. Dikes cut across beds of rock; sills push between them; laccoliths are giant blisters. Dikes may be no thicker than your finger, while laccoliths may be as big as a county. By the time we see any of these features they will already have been solid rock for many millions of years.

Volcanic Rock

Pahoe-hoe	Cindery "aa"	Bombs	Pillow lava	Columnar cooling
			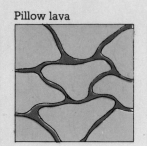	

Lava and volcanic rocks

The technical name for magma that reaches the Earth's surface is lava. Rocks formed from lava are called volcanic rocks. These tend to be fine-grained and dark in color. Lava that runs freely, cools, and solidifies with a wrinkled surface is known by the Hawaian name "pahoe-hoe." If it forms a cinder surface it is known as "aa." "Bombs" are lumps of lava ejected from the vent and solidifying very quickly. Other formations are pillow shapes – lava cooled underwater – and columns, formed by thick lava flows cooling and cracking.

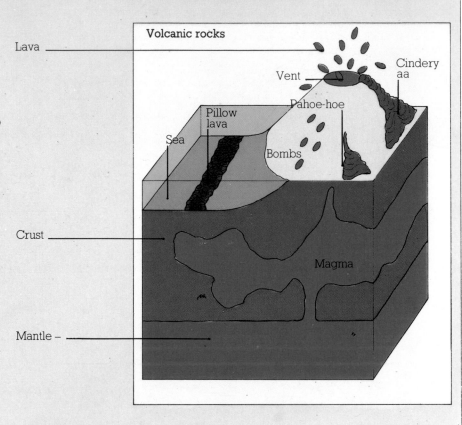

Volcanic rocks

Lava
Vent
Cindery aa
Pillow lava
Pahoe-hoe
Sea
Bombs
Crust
Magma
Mantle –

Plutonic rock

Rocks formed as magma cools and solidifies within the crust are called plutonic. They are usually lighter in color than volcanic rocks, and coarse-grained, because they cool slowly. Often the individual crystals are so large that they can be seen with the naked eye. Granite is a plutonic rock commonly found exposed on moorlands, in structures called "tors," where the overlying rocks have been worn away.

A granite "tor"

Metamorphic Rock

Rock changed by heat

Hot magma squeezing through a crack in the crust will "cook" the rock on either side. New minerals formed by the cooking action will produce a new kind of rock. The area affected can be as big as a town, around a large magma mass, or it may be small enough to be held in the palm of the hand.

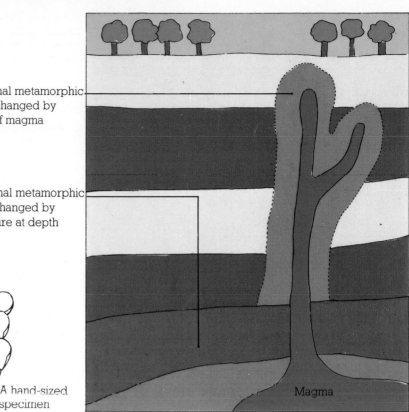

Thermal metamorphic rock changed by heat of magma

Regional metamorphic rock changed by pressure at depth

Magma

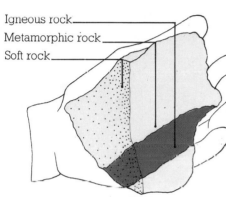

Igneous rock
Metamorphic rock
Soft rock

A hand-sized specimen

Rock changed by pressure

Rocks altered by the great stresses and pressures involved in the elaborate mountain-building processes can cover very large areas. For this reason they are called by geologists "regional metamorphic rocks." Slate is a good example of a rock that is produced as a result of pressure. The pressure has given rise to the formation of new minerals that lie within the rock, in sheets. That is why slate is easily split. Gneiss (pronounced "nice") is another common regional metamorphic rock, whose new mineral crystals are visible to the naked eye.

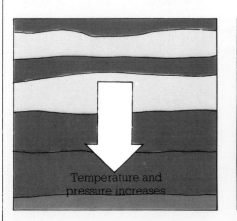

Temperature and pressure increases

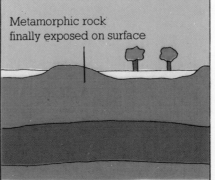

Metamorphic rock finally exposed on surface

A slate quarry

Soft Rocks

Many people have their own favorite spot for a picnic You may know of somewhere down by a river, where the water runs over the rocks and there are little sandy beaches where you can swim or just relax. If so, the next time you go there, take a closer look at the rocks, the water, and the sand. You will be witnessing something that the geologist calls "the sedimentary cycle."

Whenever a rock appears at the surface of the Earth it is destroyed. This may sound dramatic – and admittedly the process of destruction is a very long one – but it is nevertheless true. The combined action of the weather – frost, wind and rain – slowly breaks down every exposed rock, and the streams and rivers wash away the fragments. Over many millions of years whole mountain ranges can be reduced to plains just by these forces of erosion.

What happens to the broken pieces of rock that are washed away? Often they are carried long distances down rivers, or even out to sea. There the larger and more jagged pieces are broken down still further till eventually they become smooth and round. They are then washed together on beaches, or at the bottom of the sea where they become sediment – sand and mud.

In time, these sedimentary layers, or "beds," are buried beneath other, later beds, and are finally turned into beds of sedimentary rock. Much later still, the sedimentary, or soft, rocks are forced upward and folded and faulted into mountain chains. In the process some of the rocks are shot through with igneous features, and others changed to metamorphic rocks.

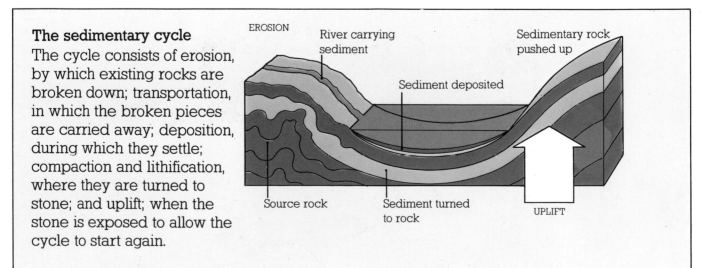

The sedimentary cycle
The cycle consists of erosion, by which existing rocks are broken down; transportation, in which the broken pieces are carried away; deposition, during which they settle; compaction and lithification, where they are turned to stone; and uplift; when the stone is exposed to allow the cycle to start again.

EROSION

River carrying sediment

Sedimentary rock pushed up

Sediment deposited

Source rock

Sediment turned to rock

UPLIFT

Erosion by water

Erosion by tree roots

Erosion by weather

Transportation of sediment

Deposition on river bed

◁ Soft rocks are broken down by the action of water, the weather, and tree roots pushing into cracks. Eventually, sediment produced by the fragments may collect as sandbanks.

Turning to Rock

Sediment is turned into sedimentary rock by two processes. Firstly, the particles are compressed and squeezed together. This squeezing action makes the particles interlock tightly with one another. Secondly, water seeping through the sediment deposits tiny crystals of mineral (such as calcite and iron oxide) between the particles, cementing them together to form a solid mass. The process is similar to the industrial manufacture of concrete, in which lumps of stone, sand and gravel are cemented together with lime.

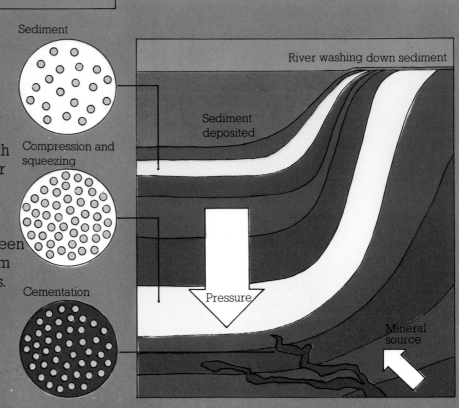

Sediment

Compression and squeezing

Cementation

River washing down sediment

Sediment deposited

Pressure

Mineral source

Types of Soft Rock

Some sedimentary rocks have a layer-like structure, in which the surfaces of the original sand or mud beds are visible. Others have no obvious layers, and can be mistaken for igneous rocks.

Splitting shale

Different sizes of rock fragment give rise to different sedimentary rocks. Layers of pebbles, as in a pebble beach, form rock called conglomerate, which looks like a pudding with raisins. Finer fragments build up sandbanks that eventually produce sandstone. Different kinds of sandstone form in rivers, seas and deserts. Desert sandstones are red and rusty-looking, while those from seas and rivers may contain fossils. The finest sediment, mud, makes a black flaky rock called shale. Sedimentary rocks formed from older rocks are called "clastic."

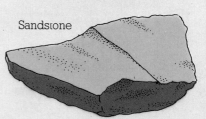

Conglomerate

Sandstone

Shale

Structures

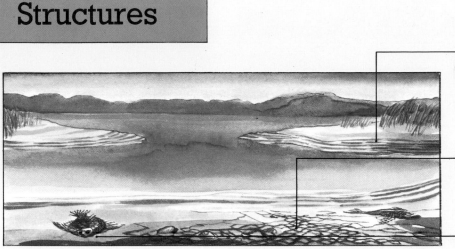

Sand ripples

Mud cracks

Fossils

Sometimes the structures in a sedimentary rock provide a glimpse of the world as it was when the sediments were laid down. In shallow water the currents produce ripples on the sandy surface. The ripple marks are sometimes preserved in the final sandstone. When a muddy pool dries up, the mud shrinks and cracks. These cracks are also discovered preserved in rock layers. The early animal life of a region can be studied from the fossils found there. Fossil land animals and plants show that the area of deposition was once near land; saltwater fish fossils show that it was once under the sea. On the other hand, freshwater shellfish fossils show that the sediments were laid down where there were originally rivers, lakes or swamps.

Biogenic Rock

Some sedimentary rocks are not made from pieces of older rocks; they are made entirely of plant and animal remains. These are called "biogenic rocks." A modern coral reef is such a rock in the making. There, the hard skeletons of the live corals build upon the skeletons of earlier corals to form a massive bed of skeletal material. Something very similar happened in the past, except that millions of years ago the skeletons need not have been of corals, but were possibly of sea lilies – animals like starfish on stalks – or of various shellfish. That

An ancient sea floor

is how limestone was formed. Chalk is a very pure form of limestone made from the skeletons of untold millions of microscopic sea creatures. Coal is a biogenic rock made of carbon from plants.

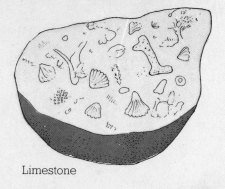

Limestone

Minerals

If you have ever seen mineral specimens in a jeweler's window, or in a case in a museum, you must have been struck by the beauty of their shape and structure. You may not have realized, however, that all the rocks found in the Earth's crust are made up of minerals such as these. Admittedly, they do not always show themselves as perfect crystals, like those on display. Some crystals are too small to be seen with the naked eye.

Every specimen of a particular mineral has the same chemical composition. A piece of the mineral quartz, found in South America, is composed of the same chemical elements, in the same proportions – one part silicon to two parts oxygen – as a piece of quartz found in Scandinavia. If those pieces had been allowed to grow freely, and to acquire more silicon and oxygen during their formation, they would have assumed a particular, and regular, shape. A mineral in this, its natural shape, is called a crystal.

In igneous rocks the crystals are sometimes well formed. The first minerals to solidify out of molten magma usually grow into their natural shapes. Those that grow later, as the melt continues to harden, have no room to form properly and so squeeze themselves in as best as they can. Sedimentary rocks do not usually show good crystal shapes.

The common rock-forming minerals make up nearly all of the Earth's crust. The economically important mineral ores, chemical compounds containing large quantities of, for instance, iron, tin, lead and uranium, are far less common.

▷ Seen here are a number of mineral specimens chosen at random from the huge selection found across the world. Some, like asbestos and sulfur, are very useful, while others, such as onyx are purely decorative. Some, like diamond and gold are both.

Cinnabar

Quartz

Crystal structure

Every igneous rock is made up of crystals of only four or five rock-forming minerals out of many hundreds. The different combinations give rise to different rocks. Granite, for instance, has crystals of the minerals feldspar, mica, quartz, and a little iron ore. The feldspars are the first to crystalize out of the molten magma and can grow into good crystal forms. The others have irregular crystal shapes.

The structure of granite

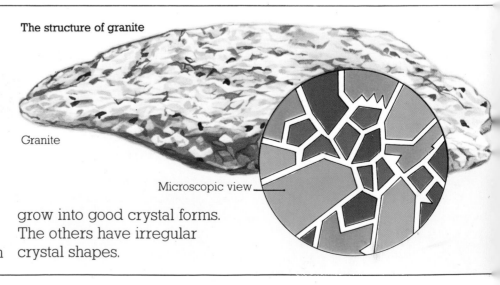

Granite

Microscopic view

24

A selection of minerals

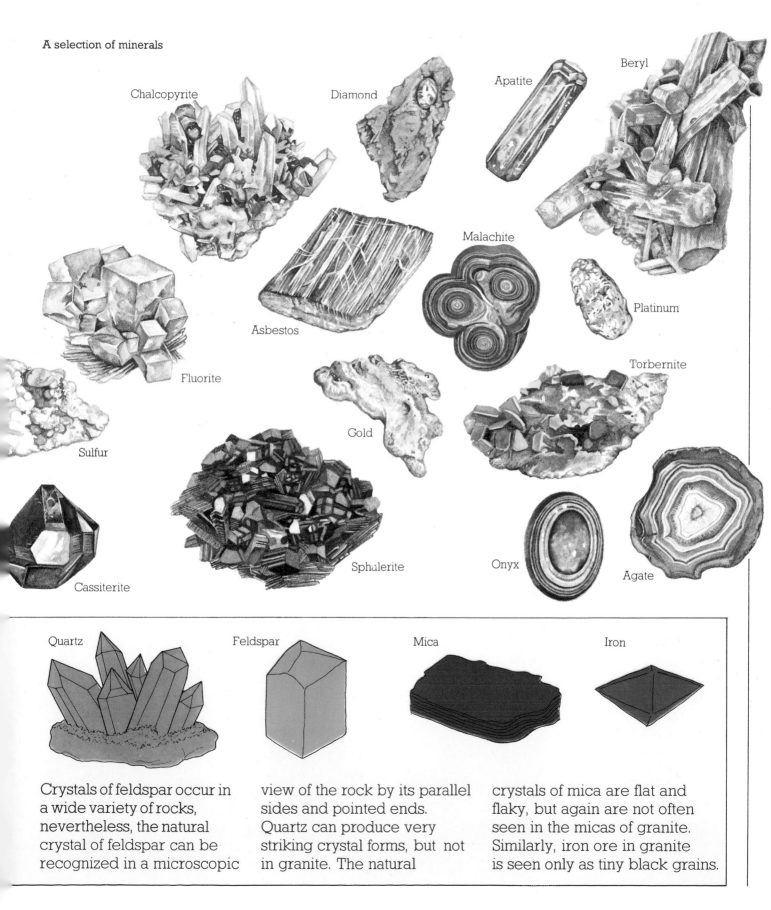

Chalcopyrite

Diamond

Apatite

Beryl

Malachite

Platinum

Asbestos

Fluorite

Torbernite

Sulfur

Gold

Cassiterite

Sphalerite

Onyx

Agate

Quartz

Feldspar

Mica

Iron

Crystals of feldspar occur in a wide variety of rocks, nevertheless, the natural crystal of feldspar can be recognized in a microscopic view of the rock by its parallel sides and pointed ends. Quartz can produce very striking crystal forms, but not in granite. The natural crystals of mica are flat and flaky, but again are not often seen in the micas of granite. Similarly, iron ore in granite is seen only as tiny black grains.

Metal Ores

Ore fields and veins

Very few of the minerals contained in the Earth's crust are economically important. These are the ore minerals. They are mined where they are concentrated by the natural processes of Earth movements and mountain building. Igneous rocks sometimes have layers of ore minerals, formed when the heavy ore minerals sank through the once-liquid magma and gathered at the bottom. More often, hot liquids and gases from the igneous body are forced into cracks in the surrounding rock, and deposit the ore minerals in veins.

Ore rich sediments

Panning for gold – as the prospectors of the last century did – involves taking some river sediment and swirling it around in a pan. Any gold particles in it will settle out first, because they are the heaviest. Much the same thing happens in nature. The fragments eroded away from a rock body are swirled around by river and sea currents. The heavy ores may settle together away from the rock-forming minerals. These deposits are called "placer" ores. They can be found on beaches, or beneath the sea. Much of the world's tin is mined from offshore placer beds in the Indian Ocean.

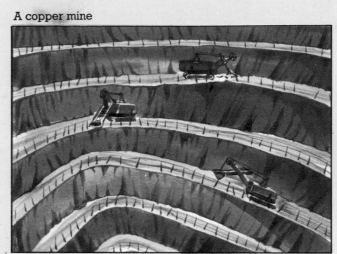

A copper mine

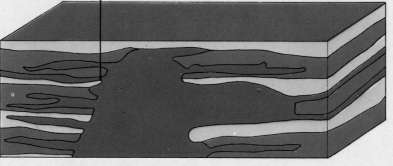

Minerals deposited along cracks in rock

Gold panning

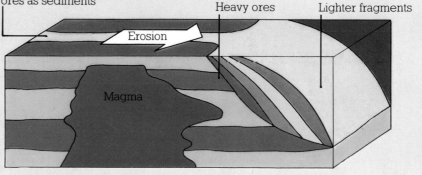

River erodes rocks and deposits ores as sediments

Erosion

Magma

Heavy ores

Lighter fragments

Mineral Tests

Because minerals do not often come in good crystal shapes, it can be difficult telling them one from another. Their color is not a reliable guide. But the color of the mark the mineral makes when it is used like a pencil *is* reliable. Iron ore gives a red streak, feldspar a grey streak. The hardness of a mineral can be found by testing to see which mineral will scratch another. Quartz will scratch a penknife, but a penknife will not scratch quartz. Minerals can also be identified by the color of the ash produced by heating with a blowpipe.

The scale of hardness

1 Talc
2 Gypsum
3 Calcite – Fingernail
4 Fluorite – copper coin
5 Apatite – window glass
6 Orthoclase – penknife
7 Quartz
8 Topaz
9 Corundum
10 Diamond

(From softest to hardest)

The heating test

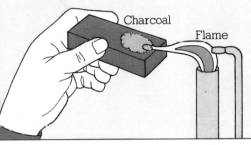

Charcoal

Flame

Heating minerals

Antimony

Bismuth

Copper

Lead

Zinc

Elements Worldwide

Oxygen is the most abundant element in the Earth's crust. Being active chemically, it is also present in most minerals. So, too, is silicon, the next most abundant element. Minerals containing both oxygen and silicon are called silicates. Metals such as iron and magnesium are quite common but are mostly found in silicates, making them too expensive to extract. Many metals are found combined only with oxygen. These include most of the ores. Some metals are found in their pure form, including copper, silver and platinum.

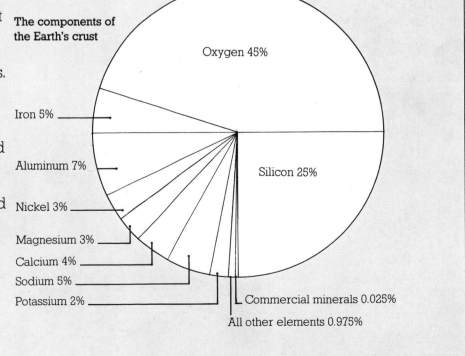

The components of the Earth's crust

Oxygen 45%

Iron 5%

Aluminum 7%

Nickel 3%

Magnesium 3%

Calcium 4%

Sodium 5%

Potassium 2%

Silicon 25%

Commercial minerals 0.025%

All other elements 0.975%

The landscapes with which we are familiar seem permanent and stable enough, but as we know they did not always look the way they do today. The surface of the Earth is constantly changing. Just imagine, a million years ago the very land where your house now stands might have been covered by glaciers! A hundred million years ago it could have been at the bottom of the sea! Go back another hundred million years and it was very likely a scorching desert, and even further back, a tropical swamp.

A prehistoric landscape of dense jungles inhabited by giant dinosaurs, such as the one shown here, would be totally unrecognizable as a place that, today, you yourself might know very well. Of course, the mountains will have long since disappeared, eroded away by the weather, and their sedimentary rocks deposited at the bottom of the sea.

What about those fossil remains in the foreground? They are evidence that about 200 million years before the dinosaurs, conditions there were very different and supported a very different kind of life. Two hundred million years is also the time span that separates us from the dinosaurs. Different animals appeared at different stages of geological time. In fact, geological periods are defined by the types of animal life that characterized them.

The so-called Cambrian period began when sea animals first developed hard skeletons. During the Devonian, animals for the first time left the sea and came to live on dry land. The Triassic period marked the beginning of the age of the dinosaurs, while the end of the Cretaceous saw the last of the dinosaurs and other large reptiles and the appearance of the first mammals. It was only at the beginning of the Pleistocene, at the start of the Ice Age, that human beings emerged. They have been on Earth for only a very short period of geological time.

▷ The presence of plant life and the dinosaurs shows that the climate at that time was quite warm. The sands gathering in the swamp will now have become sandstones, perhaps containing the fossilized bones of the dinosaurs together with other fossils of the exotic animals and vegetation that flourished alongside them.

Jurassic dinosaurs

Devonian fossil

Geological Time Scale	
Dates in millions of years ago (mya) and refer to start of geological period	
Pleistocene	2 mya
Pliocene	7 mya
Miocene	26 mya
Oligocene	38 mya
Eocene	54 mya
Palaeocene	64 mya
Cretaceous	136 mya
Jurassic	195 mya
Triassic	225 mya
Permian	280 mya
Carboniferous	345 mya
Devonian	410 mya
Silurian	440 mya
Ordovician	500 mya
Cambrian	570 mya
Precambrian	4500 mya

Passing of Time

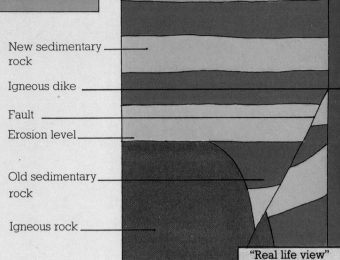

New sedimentary rock

Igneous dike

Fault

Erosion level

Old sedimentary rock

Igneous rock

When geologists look at an exposure of deformed rocks, they can identify the causes of the deformities and the order in which they occurred. In an exposure of beds of sedimentary rocks, for example, there may be igneous intrusions, breaks in the sequence and faults. An igneous intrusion cutting into sedimentary beds must have done so after the beds were laid down. At a later date the whole sequence may have been eroded to a plain, and new sedimentary beds built up on top. A break in the sequence that cuts across the beds and the intrusion must have come after both. If a fault cuts the beds, intrusion, and break in sequence, then it followed all three. A dike cutting right across everything else has been emplaced last. The rule is that if one feature cuts across another, then that feature is the younger.

"Real life view"

Changes with time

1 Sedimentary rock

2 Igneous rock forced up

3 Erosion and upthrust occurs

4 New sediments form on top

5 Fault appears

6 Dike – magma forced up

Index Fossils

Fossils that can be used to date the rock in which they are found are called index fossils. Fossils of the shelled, octopus-like ammonites are one example. Knowing when the different species lived enables geologists to determine when a rock containing ammonite fossils was laid down. For instance, a rock containing a fossil of the ammonites *Hildoceras* must have been formed between 170 and 200 million years ago; one containing a fossil of *Sagenites* between 190 and 220 million years ago. Thus a rock containing both must have formed between 190 and 200 million years ago.

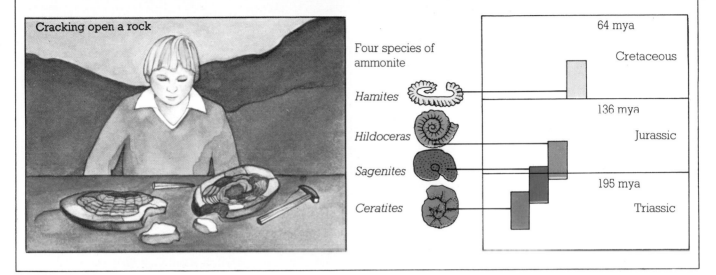

Cracking open a rock

Four species of ammonite

Hamites

Hildoceras

Sagenites

Ceratites

64 mya	Cretaceous
136 mya	Jurassic
195 mya	Triassic

Tracing Ice Ages

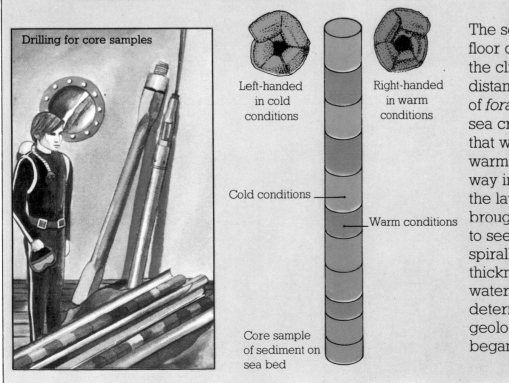

Drilling for core samples

Left-handed in cold conditions

Right-handed in warm conditions

Cold conditions

Warm conditions

Core sample of sediment on sea bed

The sediments of the sea floor can tell us much about the climatic changes of the distant past. Certain species of *foraminifera* – microscopic sea creatures – have shells that will spiral one way in warm water and the other way in cold. We can examine the layers of sea sediment, brought up by core samplers, to see where the left- or right-spiralled shells occur. The thickness of the layers of cold water shells enable us to determine when the geologically recent Ice Ages began and ended.

Fossils

A mammoth with its meat still edible, preserved in frozen mud in Siberia.

Not all fossils have been turned to stone. Basically, a fossil is the remains of an extinct animal or plant found preserved in the ground, whose presence tells us about local conditions at some period in the geological past. Some fossils, such as the frozen mammoth or an insect caught in amber, retain most of the creature's original body material. In others, there may be no body material left, as with cast or trace fossils. There are also other types of fossil, between these two extremes, with varying amounts of the original body material preserved.

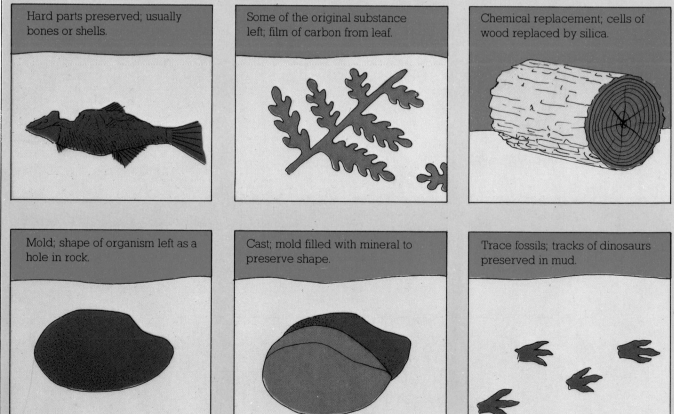

Hard parts preserved; usually bones or shells.

Some of the original substance left; film of carbon from leaf.

Chemical replacement; cells of wood replaced by silica.

Mold; shape of organism left as a hole in rock.

Cast; mold filled with mineral to preserve shape.

Trace fossils; tracks of dinosaurs preserved in mud.

Fossil Evidence for Evolution

Evolution is the changing of plant and animal life into new and different forms at different periods of time. Its progress is often charted in the fossil record of the Earth's rocks. In the Upper Cretaceous period, 120-65 million years ago, the development of the horned dinosaurs, the ceratopsians, can be traced from lightly built two-legged creatures to the massive armoured beasts at the end of the Age of Reptiles. Similarly, fossils show that it took 65 million years for human beings to evolve from small tree shrews, through lemur-like and ape-like creatures.

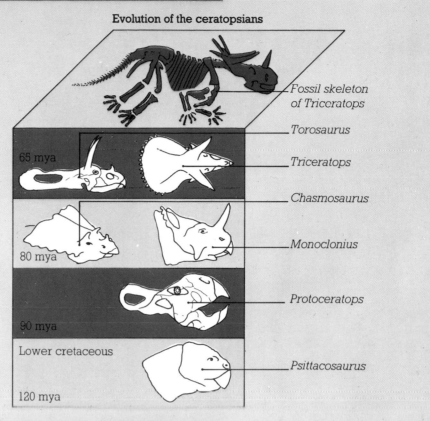

Evolution of the ceratopsians

Fossil skeleton of Triceratops

Torosaurus

Triceratops

Chasmosaurus

Monoclonius

Protoceratops

Psittacosaurus

65 mya

80 mya

90 mya

Lower cretaceous

120 mya

The Moving World of Fossils

About 250 million years ago all the continents were joined together in one enormous supercontinent that geologists call Pangaea. How do we know this? One of the most important lines of evidence is the fossil record of each continent. Fossils of the same fern-like plants and land-living reptiles have been found in 250-million-year-old rocks as far apart as Africa, India and South America. These plants and animals could not have traveled over water, and so the whole must have comprised one great land mass.

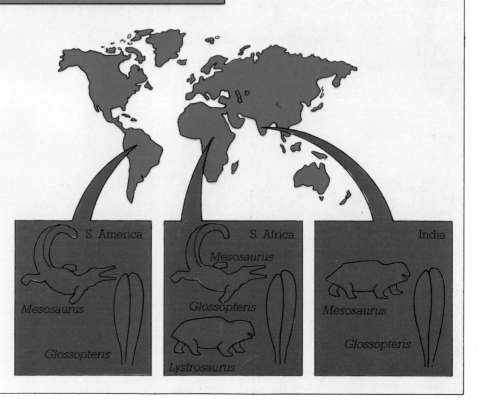

S. America

Mesosaurus

Glossopteris

S. Africa

Mesosaurus

Glossopteris

Lystrosaurus

India

Mesosaurus

Glossopteris

Economic Geology

If you look out of a high window down onto an urban landscape, you will find it very hard to pick out anything that does not ultimately come from minerals in the ground. The surrounding buildings are likely to be of concrete, made from limestone, or of bricks, from clay, or of steel, from iron ore. The glass of the window panes is made from sand, the tarmac road surfaces from oil. Plastics, too, are made from oil. Wood and vegetable products owe their existence to the geological processes of erosion that form the soil in which the trees once grew. This soil contains minerals that supply the chemicals needed to sustain growth.

So important to us are the raw materials we draw from the Earth that we count the early stages of our history by them. We refer to the Old Stone Age, the New Stone Age, the Bronze Age, the Iron Age, and so on.

Nowadays whole industries are based on winning building stone from the limestones and sandstones of the mountains, metals from the igneous and sedimentary ores, and coal, oil and natural gas – our main sources of power – from deposits underground or beneath the sea. Nuclear power is produced from uranium, which is itself a metal ore.

All these resources are finite, and have been laid down over hundreds of millions of years. They are not found everywhere on Earth, and many are rapidly being used up. This is a cause of growing concern.

In a hundred years' time our cityscape will look very different from the way it does today. But on a geological time scale this city will be very short-lived anyway. The land on which it is built will one day be at the bottom of the sea or at the top of a high mountain! We will all be fossils by then!

▷ Even the choice of a successful location of a city will depend upon geological factors. Only certain kinds of rocks, for instance, are strong enough to support a city's foundations. The natural landscape is important too. There are many examples of cities built on hills for protection, or by rivers for trading purposes.

Glass

Gravel

Gasoline

Tar

Brick

Iron

Cement

◁ Rocks and minerals are the subjects of geology and the servants of the modern world. A close look at a city will show how human beings have exploited the riches of nature for the sake of their immediate needs.

Coal, Oil and Gas

Coal, oil, and gas are fossil fuels. Their energy is energy from the Sun, absorbed by plants millions of years ago and preserved in their remains and in those of the animals that consumed them. Coal was formed in tropical swamps, where dead trees and ferns piled up in shallow pools but did not rot away completely. Oil and gas were made from the juices of extinct tiny sea-creatures. Long after they had been buried and the sediments turned to stone, the oil and gas separated from the rest and floated upward through tiny pores in the rock.

Eventually, they became trapped below a layer of rock through which they could not pass. So coal is mined where it is formed, but oil and gas are not.

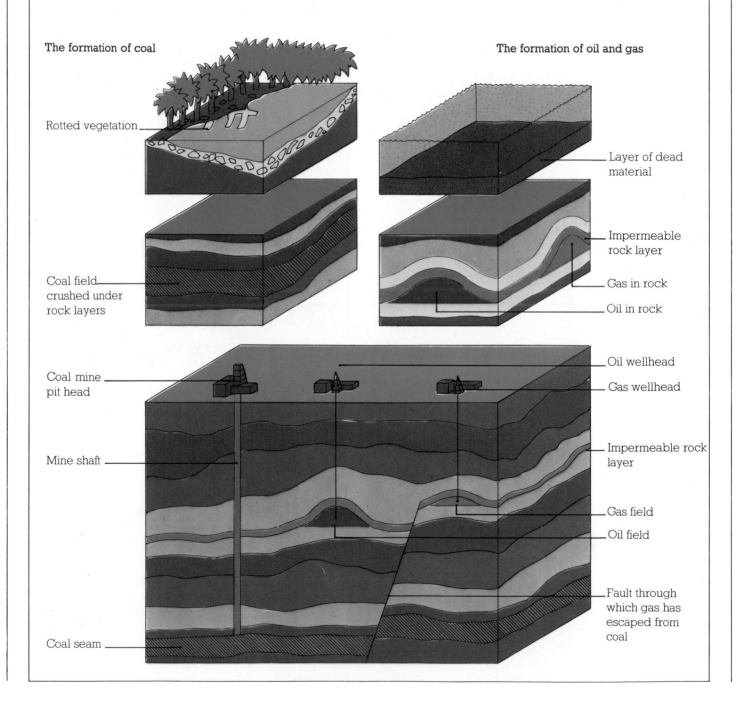

The formation of coal

Rotted vegetation

Coal field crushed under rock layers

The formation of oil and gas

Layer of dead material

Impermeable rock layer

Gas in rock

Oil in rock

Coal mine pit head

Mine shaft

Coal seam

Oil wellhead

Gas wellhead

Impermeable rock layer

Gas field

Oil field

Fault through which gas has escaped from coal

The Products of Oil

Oil is our most versatile form of energy. It not only provides power for heating and lighting but is also the basis of a vast number of manufactured products, from plastics to fertilizers. Some of our clothes and shoes thus began as plants and animals from earlier geological periods. Because our supplies of coal, and particularly of oil and gas, are limited, other sources of energy are now being tried. These include nuclear power and solar, wind, wave, and water power.

Plexiglass

Nylon

Plastics

Tires

Fertilizer

Weed killer

Paint

Rocks and Minerals

Some of the minerals and rocks that are useful to us may be used more or less as we find them. These include salt, slate, and gravel, and the building stones for our houses. Others have first to go through complicated refining processes. The metal ores, for instance, have to be heated to extremely high temperatures to give pure metals; and silica sand must be melted down before it can be turned into glass. Similarly, some minerals and rocks are found on Earth's surface; for others we must dig deep underground.

1 Clay
2 Slate
3 Glass
4 Stone
5 Gypsum
6 Salt
7 Pigments
8 Gravel
9 Asbestos
10 Magnesium
11 Phosphates
12 Iron
13 Copper
14 Tin

Glossary

Continental crust   The part of the Earth's crust that forms the continents. It is made of rock lighter than that of the oceanic crust and floats on it.

Crust   The outermost layer of Earth.

Deposition   The accumulation of pebbles, sand or mud at the bottom of the sea or on a river bed.

Erosion   The wearing away of exposed rocks by the action of the weather or by streams and sea waves.

Fault   A crack in the rock layers of Earth's crust. It is caused by rocks (at each side of the crack) that have moved against one another at some time in the past.

Fold   A curved, wave-like structure in the rock layers of the crust, formed by the layers being pushed up together while mountains are being built.

Fossil   The trace of an ancient animal or plant found preserved in a rock.

Hard rock   Geologist's term for any igneous or metamorphic rock.

Igneous rock   A rock that has formed from hot molten material which has cooled and hardened, either underground or on the surface of the Earth.

Lava   Magma, the molten rock material from the depths of the Earth, that has broken through to the surface in a volcano. Lava can also be used to describe the igneous rock formed as the molten material hardens.

Magma   The hot molten material that is found at places beneath the Earth's surface. When it solidifies it becomes igneous rock.

Metamorphic rock   A rock that has formed when a previously existing rock has been changed by great heat or great pressure.

Mineral   A naturally formed substance with a fixed chemical composition, found in the Earth.

Oceanic crust   The part of Earth's crust that forms the beds of the oceans.

Plutonic rock   An igneous rock that solidified underground.

Regional metamorphism   The production of a metamorphic rock from an existing rock by great pressure.

Sedimentary rock   A rock formed from the deposition of fragments, such as pebbles, sand or mud, and their lithification deep underground.

Soft rock   Geologist's term for any sedimentary rock.

Volcanic rock   An igneous rock that solidified on the surface of the earth.

Index

PRINTED IN BELGIUM BY
proost
INTERNATIONAL BOOK PRODUCTION